The Essential
Smudge Guide Book

Twirling Thunderbird

CONTENTS

ACKNOWLEDGMENTS
To the Creator

Father Sky

Mother Earth

Spiritual Beings

Spiritual Helpers

All my Relations.

Thank you for your guidance and knowledge

DEDICATIONS

To the Great Mystery

I was once told that knowledge

is to be shared with all Nations.

We all as People, all have the capacity to be Earth People.

Let us reconnect to the Creators Path.

Let us have the wisdom to live in harmony with our fellow brothers and sisters.

May we realize our balance with our environment and all the Spiritual Beings
upon Mother Earth.

We seek Reconnection and finding our Spiritual Inner Self.

This is essential to preserving our place within Mother Earth.

To my Wife Yellow Butterfly

You make Life worth living.

FOREWARD

It has been told to me ~ That long ago People would often Smudge very early in the morning facing the Rising Grandfather Sun to the East Wind. They would often seek out where Water met the Sky, at a lake or river. When the Sunrise was halfway on the horizon; This is the Sacred time they would Smudge, when a representation of both the Spirit World and this World would meet. Where Water met the Sky, where Darkness now turned to Light, where Spiritual Dreamworld met with this World. It was at this Sacred time, at this half way meeting, that there is a special connection to Self and the Creator.

Within this book I offer my personal advice and views towards the Sacred Smudging Ceremony.

Expressing the Creators Gifts to find greater meaning and happiness in life.

To seek balance within the Traditional Medicine Wheel to receive Physical health, Emotional health, Spiritual health and Mental well-being.

To honor the Gifts of the Gitche Manitou - Great Mystery through sharing and strengthening our connection to our Environment and our fellow Spiritual Beings.

There are many Nations from different Territories, with many Customs that have their own unique protocols and methods when it comes to Sacred Smudge Ceremony.

For centuries many Cultures have used smudging as a way to create a cleansing smoke bath that is used to purify the body, aura, energy, ceremonial/ritual spaces or any other space and personal articles.

I offer here, my own unique perspective on Sacred Smudge Ceremony. This book is by no means a full definition or representation of Native American Sacred Smudging.

Every Nation of Peoples have their own unique traditions and personal preferences. I present this book as a general guide and to put across my personal view on Smudge Ceremony.

I believe Ceremonial Smudge will always bring Goodness as long as it comes from the Heart with good intentions.

We are all born with Gifts from the Creator. I believe to share our Gifts with others is the Key to personal Fulfillment and Happiness.

As a Society, we seek our collective Spiritual Reconnection to Ourselves, our fellow Spiritual Beings and our Environment. Not just for us, but for future generations.

Twirling Thunderbird

Thank You ~ Meegwetch

SMUDGE CEREMONY ITEMS

The Items that are used in Ceremony

Items in the Smudging Ceremony may have representation within the Four Winds of the Medicine Wheel.

Representations of Ceremonial Medicine.

Abalone Shell – The Abalone shell or clay bowl represents Feminine Powers within The Healing Waters.

Feather – Which represents the Air. The Breath of Life. Messenger of Prayer. The feather and wind it creates represent air.

Sacred Plants – Tobacco, Sage, Cedar and Sweet Grass, The herbs and resins represent the Earth.

Fire - The Flame used to ignite the herbs represents fire. Preferably utilize wooden or Natural Fire material such as wooden matches.

Plants used in Smudging

The most common Plants used in Native American Smudge are Sweet grass, Tobacco, Cedar and Sage.

I will mention them in further detail in this chapter.

It is recommended for the strongest outcomes and effects to use the Local Plants of the area you are in.

The Plant has from the Local area is more Synchronized with the Land from which it is from.

Smudge Sticks

Smudge Sticks can be put together from fresh or dried Herbs and Flowers.

Fresh Plants are recommended because of the flexibility they have when tying the bundles.

After this they may be dried for 3 to 5 days.

You can now Layer your Plants together and begin shaping your bundle.

Using a cotton string. Tie your bundle at the top and start wrapping around the bundle spiraling downward. Tuck in any loose stems on the way.

After lighting you may fan with a Feather or Fan the Smudge Stick on its own.

Tie and Trim any excess string.

List of Common Smudge Stick Plants

Dried plants that are tied into bundles are called smudge sticks, which are lit and burned on one end. Loose plants can be burned in the shell or bowl or placed directly onto burning wood or crumbled over a piece of charcoal.

Red Cedar

Native cultures use the smoke of Red Cedar for purification and healing ceremonies.

Palo Santo

Palo Santo is a mystical tree that grows on the coast of South America. In Spanish, the name literally means "Holy Wood" and is best when used when deep healing and clearing energies are needed. It is part of the citrus family and has sweet notes of pine, mint and a lemon citrus- like scent.

It is often used to cure the symptoms of emotional trauma, stress, colds, headaches, inflammation.

Palo Santo creates a pleasant, fresh smoke used commonly in Ecuador and Peru. It provides an uplifting scent that raises your vibration in preparation for meditation and allows for a deeper connection to the Source of all creation. Palo Santo enhances creativity and brings forth good fortune to those who are open to its Energies.

Lavender

You can burn lavender petals along with the stems. Lavender has a sweet scent of Blue and Desert sage. Lavender along with Cedar can help with a restful night's sleep as well as alleviate bad dreams. Lavender also promotes relaxation and positive emotions to put you in a good mood.

Mixing Sage with Other Herbs

Sage is the most commonly used method of smudging and you can mix your Sage with a variety of other Herbs as well.

Sage

Cleansing, Balance, and Strengthening.

The smoke from sage to use to cleanse, bless and heal, remove negativity from an object or to purify the person being cleansed .Sage comes in a variety of many different types and scents. White Sage, Common Sage to Desert Sage, Desert and Loaded sage mixes are excellent for woody and sweet scents.

White sage

Known far and wide for protection and purification. White sage is known for its properties as a Body Purifier. Native Americans have used White Sage for centuries for clearing negative energies of Purifying spaces, people or objects.

Desert Sage

Desert sage, (desert rose) is the favorable option to using White Sage. This Sage holds the same cleansing Energy as white sage although the scent is uniquely different. Desert sage is used to repel bad feelings and influences.

This Sage holds its burning power for longer smudges when in a bundle.

Aspen

The essential oils in the leaves work to alleviate anxiety. Aspen burns quickly. Sometimes it's preferred to add Aspen essential oils in Sage Smudge Sprays. Aspen is known to be used traditionally for protection.

Rosemary

Rosemary removes negative energy from places and spaces. Rosemary is known to be added into a mix with Sage Bundles. Rosemary is soothing and encourages a sense of peace when used within your Space.

Lemongrass

Lemongrass is also known to have an energizing scent and is refreshing and helps with Clarity and Focus. Lemongrass is purifying and cleansing.

Cinnamon

Cinnamon increases Energy and Motivation and promotes healing. Burning cinnamon can be used if you have a cold or flu. The essential oils in cinnamon help relax, soothe you and can put you in a good mood.

Blue Spruce

Blue Spruce has a very smooth scent and is known to be used for cleansing purposes to promote Serenity and Grace.

Cedar

Cedar is known to be used commonly with white sage. Cedar is commonly used in Native American Rituals and Ceremonies. Traditionally, Cedar has been for Renewal and Protection and positive Dreams.

Bay Leaves

The Bay leaf is used for Protection, Healing and for Anxiety. The Essential oil in bay leaves is known to work as a mood enhancer.

Eucalyptus

Eucalyptus isn't just used as a great decongestant during cold season and known for muscle relief in bath products, Smudging with eucalyptus is for protection, health boosting as well as being energising for cleansings.

Myrrh

The Oil and Resin alike is known for having an earthy woodsy scent. Myrrh is known for perception and healing.

Peppermint

Peppermint puts forth a refreshing and smooth scent

Pine

Pine needles are often used to bless a new home. Pine is an excellent herb for cleansing and protection. Often it is used in Healthy Teas by Native Americans. Pine is associated with strength and good health.

Catnip

Catnip was burned for love, grace, sharing, beauty, and happiness within the home or sacred space.

Clove

The Psychic Plant, this herb is known as a Psychic enhancer. It is also used to produce Spiritual vibrations and to purify the area and to drive away bad Spirits when used with Sweet Grass.

Dandelion

The properties of dandelion are associated with the warm Air of the Summer. Dandelion is well known as a Healing Plant. Has very strong Feminine Powers.

Ginger

Ginger is a powerful protective Plant. Known for its Healing Energy. All Plants that Heal have powerful vibrational Energy.

Chamomile

Chamomile is used in many Organic Bath products, The oils are best in Smudge Sprays along with other herbs for happiness and comfort.

Thyme

Thyme is an excellent for overcoming emotional obstacles, creativity and as a memory booster.

Liac

Lilac has a soothing, relaxing and scent.

Amaranth

Amaranth promotes intuition and adds comfort to unfamiliar spaces.

Mugwort

Mugwort when mixed with dried Sage is sometimes called Black Sage. The mugwort plant brings forth clarity and strengthens intuitive abilities.

Herbs for Smudging

There are many herbs for smudging. The Vibrational Energy of the Plants draws Healing Energies from the Astral Plane.

Juniper leaves	Yarrow leaves/flowers
Pine Needles	Labrador Tea leaves
White Spruce Pitch	Pearly Everlasting leaves/flowers
Pepperwood leaves	Agelica Root
Cow Parsnip roots/leaves	Bear Root - Osha Root
Lavender	Copal
Sagebrush	Frankincense
Myrrh	Incense-cedar mistletoe

Herbs for Smudging - Essential Oils

North American Natives used aromatic oils for smudges.

Smudging Rituals and aromatic plant based herbal remedies. These herbal extracts are referred to as 'Essential Oils'.

Dried Mugwort ~ keeps a fire smoldering for a long time. Mugwort is used as a sacred smoking or smudging herb for protection or divination.

Desert Lavender ~ is an aromatic herb used in smudging and cleansing rituals.

Yellow Birch ~ made by the bark of a tree and used in Smudging Rituals

Carrot seed ~ from the dried seed of the wild carrot

Cedar Leaf ~ from the fresh leaves and twigs of the Thuja, a slow-growing, narrow conifer.

Balsam Fir ~ from the needles and twigs of the northeast American balsam fir tree and used in Smudging Rituals

Juniper Berry ~ the scent is from the ripe berries and used by Native Americans for smudging, purification and healing

Bitter Orange ~ from the peel of a tree. Used to help uplift moods and relieve stress in Smudging Rituals

Peppermint ~ from the leaves and top of the herb and used in Smudging Rituals

Spearmint ~ from the fresh flowering tops.

Wintergreen ~ from the wild-crafted leaves

> **Wormwood** ~ from the dried leaves and flowers of the plant.

Meaning behind Ceremonial Plants and Items

- o **Everything has Two Sides**
- o **Sacred Plants have a Physical side and as well as a Spiritual side.**
- o **Plants have Medicinal aspects on the Physical side.**
- o **Plants also possess Healing aspects on the Spiritual side.**
- o **Plants also have Ceremonial and Cultural purposes.**

Abalone Shell

The Abalone shell or clay bowl represents The Healing Waters.

The reflected sunlight on the Abalone Shell projects the Creators Energy.

It is said that the Creator speaks to us on the reflected rays of light from the Abalone Shell. We regard Light as the Creators voice.

We look the Spiritual West from which the Thunderbirds bring forth Waters.

Tobacco

East Spirit – Medicine of the East Wind.

Gifted from the Sun Spirit to the People to carry our Prayers directly to the Creator.

Sacred plant of Prayer, the Tobacco strengthens our Prayers.

Tobacco signifies Gratefulness and Thankfulness to the Creator.

Tobacco is always offered before picking medicines. When you offer tobacco to a plant and explain your reasons for being there, the plant will let all the plants in the area know your intentions and why you are picking them,

Sage

South Spirit – Medicine of the South Wind.

Considered the Feminine or the Medicine of Women.

Is seen as a women's medicine, and offers strength, wisdom, and clarity of purpose.

It is used to symbolize the life-giving power of women.
Sage is often braided into three strands, similar to Sweetgrass, and hung within one's home.

It may be tied with a ribbon in one of the colors of the medicine wheel: Red, yellow, black, white or green.

Having qualities of patience, understanding, harmonious, good judgment, tolerance, empathy and good leadership.

Considered to have attributes of Emotional maturity, Love, Romance, and promotion of harmonious relationships.

Represents

Purity of Heart.

Gentle Intuition towards others.

Adventurous, Spontaneous and Passion.
Promotes meditative healing.

Emotional Trust and Faith.

Feminine Power and confidence.

Spiritual closeness to Mother Earth and the Creator.

The Male strives to achieve the Female qualities of Compassion,
Humility, Sharing and Fortitude.

Cedar

West Spirit – Medicine of the West Wind.

We look to the West Spirit for Spiritual Knowledge, Prayer and Healing.

We seek Spiritual connection and Guidance.

The Spirit of the protector Thunderbird nests in the boughs of the Cedar trees and like the Thunderbird; Cedar protects us from negativity.

The Cedar plant calms our Dreams and grounds our thoughts of worry.

Attracts positive energy, feelings, emotions and for balance.

Commonly used to Purify the home.

Cedar strengthens our connection to our ancestors.

Cedar represents the application of Wisdom.

Reminds us to take time for Introspection.

Sweet Grass

North Spirit – Medicine of the North Wind.

Braided Sweet Grass is often thought of as the Hair of Mother Earth.

The Sweet Grass Braid, like the braids we adorn, represents our Spiritual connection to Mother Earth and all the Creators Spiritual Beings.

The Sweet smell of Sweet Grass is utilized to cleanse your space or environment of negative Spiritual Energies and is very protective.

It is often thought of as the first Plant gifted and to grow on Mother Earth.

Grass reminds us to have perseverance in times of great adversity.

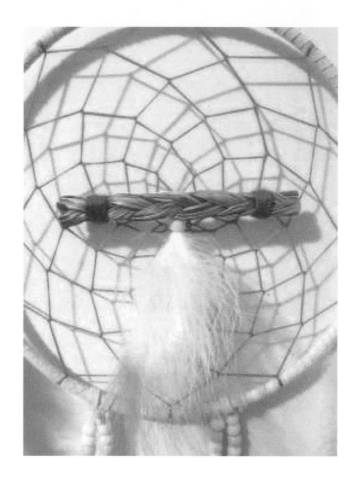

To have clarity, focus and organization of the Mind.
We are to conserve and not waste precious resources, whatever they
may be.

Strengthens our Intellectual Beliefs; our concerns for Human Justice and
Freedom.

To meditate, self-reflect and contemplate on the important things in our
lives. We can then give proper priorities to what really matters: those we
love around us.

Sweet grass is the sacred hair of Mother Earth and its sweet aroma reminds people of the gentleness, love and kindness she has for the people.

Native people pick it and braid it in 3 strands representing love, kindness and honesty.

Sweet grass is used for smudging and purification of the spirit; when Sweet grass is used in a healing or talking circle it has a calming effect.

It is said that Sweet grass attracts the good Spirit, so use it to call in the Spirit.

Representation of the Feather

Air originates from the Spirit of the South Wind.

The Feather and wind it creates represent Spirit of the Air from the South Wind.

It is the Air we are first Gifted and we give our last Air when we go onto the next Cycle of Life.

This is the Breath of Life. There is Spiritual Power within the Air.

The Feather carries the Spiritual attributes of the bird within it.

Feather is a Messenger of Prayer.

Representation of Fire

The Flame used to ignite the herbs represents the Element of Fire.

Fire originates from the Spirit of the North Wind.

Smoke from the Fire cleanses the body of scents and negative Energies picked up during the day.

The sight, sound and scent of Fire will clean your senses.

The Healing Power of the Creator is passed to the Four Corners of the Universe.

Grandfather Sun transfers the Creators Energy to the Four Corners of Mother Earth.

The Creators Energy now enters the Plant World.

The Spirit of Fire now releases the Pure Energy of the Creator to Heal and Cleanse.

Because sacrifice was made for us to be gifted Fire. We have Gratitude when lighting Fire.

SMUDGE CEREMONY MEANING

Spiritual - *To Smudge is to walk with The Creator, our Ancestors, the Spiritual Helpers, Father Sky, Mother Earth, our Relatives and all other People and Creatures of the Earth, - in a good way - that honors our Spirit and the Creator.*

A Sacred means of Healing and Purification by the Natural Power of the Creator.

To create the proper mindset and atmosphere to promote healing and welcome positive Spiritual Powers.

We Smudge to promote healthy living. We are mindful of what we take into our body. We are mindful of the Law of Attraction. That when we put out positive Energy into the Universe, we will attract positive Energy back to ourselves.

We Smudge in times of sickness. Having a Positive mindset is paramount in the promotion of healing. Laughter and a positive atmosphere is often the best medicine. Surround yourself with positive happy people. It is a time we call upon our Spiritual Helpers for help and guidance.

In times of Ceremony we Smudge before and after to Purify Space of any lingering toxic Energies and set our positive Mindset.

Give and Take. The Plants give themselves just as the Animals, just as Mother Earth, to help us live. We too can Give by sharing our Gifts with others and making this World a better place.

Focus on our Intention within our Prayer.

To be clear on what is needed in our life or for a loved one.

When we Smudge, we wash away impurities of sadness, anxiety, negative thoughts.

To purify any unwanted toxic energies, feeling, thoughts, emotions or Spirits that may be lingering onto a space or person.

Cleanse our Minds
Positive Intent

To have good thoughts – To have a positive outlook on the day. (To put us in a Positive frame of Mind for the Day ahead and have a Positive outlook towards it.

To have a Positive outlook for ourselves, People around us, to our Interactions with the Environment.

To seek the Underlying goodness in People – To see the "Goodness" in their Actions.

Clear our Eyes

We smudge our Eyes to see the goodness in things.

To have our Eyes See the good things in a person.

To see goodness in other peoples actions.

To see the goodness in People and our Situations.

We smudge our Mouth

To Speak good things to Others with good intentions.

To give People the "Benefit of the Doubt".

To say the things that are hard to say

To speak with Truth from the Heart.

To put forth Positive Vibrations into the Universe
 as to receive Positive Energy.

What we Speak matters – To speak Positive makes us feel better
- we call this Good Medicine.

We smudge our Space to Clear the Air around us

To Purify the Space…To clear the way for Positive Vibrational Energy to enter the space. To promote positive - Feelings, Thoughts, Attitudes, Spirits.

To clear space of Negative toxic Energies that Linger in the Spiritual Realm. (this should be done before and after every Ceremony)

Utilized in the Home, Healing Lodge, Ceremonial places and Sacred Items or anyplace needed.

**We smudge our Ears
to Hear the good words in a Person**

To Hear goodness in the other Persons words spoken.(To Hear good things in others).

To Hear the goodness in People when they speak their words.

So that our ears will hear the spiritual truths given us by our Creator.

To Hear the words are in the right place and coming from the Heart.

We smudge our Heart.

To feel empathy and compassion for other people.

To be receptive to how the other person feels.

To express only the goodness in ourselves towards others.

We cleanse our hearts so that our hearts will feel the truth, grow with us in harmony and balance, be good and pure, be open to show compassion, gentleness, empathy and caring for others.

We smudge our feet

to clear any negativity clinging to us.

By smudging our feet, we can imagine walking in another's shoes. We can more readily emphasize with others and have understanding.

We Smudge our feet to clear any lingering Negative Energies from where we have walked.

We cleanse our feet so that our feet will seek to walk the true path.

To seek balance and harmony, to lead us closer to our families, friends, community.

We walk closer to our loved ones and help us flee our enemies, and lead us closer to the Creator.

The Power of Positive Vibrational output

We believe that positive Energies we put forth into the Universe we shall be received back to us. This Karma or Positive Feedback is sometimes known as the Law of Attraction.

Putting forth positive Power into our environment promotes healing and well- being for us and others.

Positive Energy is contagious and is the driving force for activities we enjoy.

Power of Silence and Positive Space

Silent places are Sacred places.

It is often said that the only noise to be heard in Prayer is the sounds of Nature.

Our Prayers are heard most clearly and with most impact when spoken in Silent Spaces.

Power of a Positive Mindset

Resetting and starting your day with a positive Mindset has many positive side effects.

Before Smudging we can prepare our minds by focusing on the Intent of our Prayer. Focus on what is specifically needed for ourselves and our loved ones.

PROCEDURES

Individual Ceremony Procedures

Circle Ceremony Procedures

Home Ceremony Procedures

Individual Ceremony Procedures

Lay Table/cloth on the Ground or on Table and place Items on top.

It is Protocol to brush cloth clean with palm of hands, before and after use to clean cloth and to not shake out cloth. Keep in mind the Cloth itself may have Sacred properties.

Open window or door slightly to let out negative energies.

Place Sacred Plants into the Abalone Shell.
      Note (Plants can be used together or on their own)
   (Meaning behind Ceremonial Medicine and Items)
   Sage - Cedar - Sweet Grass - Tobacco

Sage is most commonly placed first.

Medicines to be placed on Tablecloth or on Ground.

Prayer of Thanks performed quietly or spoken out.

Wooden Matches are used to light the Sacred Smudge. (I will mention that Matches are to be shaken out and not blown.)

The Feather is Smudged in the Smoke to Bless and Recognize the Feathers Spirit.

The Feather is now used to Stoke the ambers. (To be fanned side to side and not up and down.)

The Individual can now Smudge themselves by using the hands to guide Smoke onto themselves.

Feet – Legs - Body

Head – Mouth – Eyes - Ears

A personal Sacred Prayer can now be said. You can say it out loud, whisper or Pray silently.

Smoke rises, our prayers rise to the Spirit World where the Grandfathers and our Creator reside.

The Feather is now Smudged (cleansed) again and put away.

Negative energy, feelings, and emotions are lifted away.

The remaining Medicine is allowed to cool and is returned to Mother Earth at the base of a Tree representing the Tree of Life, with Gratitude and Respect by Giving Thanks.

Circle Ceremony Procedures

A competent Person is chosen to Facilitate.
Lay Tablecloth on the Ground. A small table can also be set up with a Tablecloth covering.

(It is protocol to brush cloth clean with hands, before and after use to clean cloth and to not shake out cloth. Keep in mind the Cloth itself may have Sacred properties.)

Open window or door slightly to let out negative energies.

An Abalone Shell or Bowl is usually used to place Plant Medicines into.

Place Sacred Plant(s) into the Abalone Shell.

Sage - Cedar - Sweet Grass - Tobacco

(Plants can be used together or on their own although Sage is the most commonly utilized.)

Medicines to be placed on Tablecloth or on Ground.

The Sacred Smudge is Prayed upon by the Individual.

Wooden Matches are used to light the Sacred Smudge. (I will mention that Matches are to be shaken out and not blown.)

The Feather is Smudged in the Smoke to Bless and Recognize the Feathers Spirit.

The Feather is now used to Stoke the ambers.(to be fanned side to side and not up and down.)

All Participants (Elder First) are Smudged one at a time.

Fan the ambers lightly with Feather side to side.
(Try not to stoke Bowl directly in front of Participant. Stoke first then bring shell close to Person).

Allow the *Person* to Smudge themselves by using their hands to guide Smoke onto themselves.

Feet - Legs - Body

Head – Mouth – Eyes - Ears

Present the Smudge Bowl to each Person in a clockwise fashion.

Return back to Tablecloth to Place Feather.

The *Facilitator* can now Smudge themselves by using the hands to guide Smoke onto themselves.

Feet – Legs - Body
Head – Mouth – Eyes - Ears

Negative energy, feelings, and emotions are lifted away.

***The Feather is now Presented to the Elder or Person chosen to say a Sacred Prayer* * that can now be said. Prayer can be said out loud, whispered or Prayed silently. (Sometimes a Teaching may accompany a Prayer).

The Feather is now Smudged (cleansed) again and put away.

The remaining Medicine is allowed to cool and is returned to Mother Earth at the base of a Tree representing the Tree of Life, with Gratitude and Respect by Giving Thanks.

Home Ceremony Procedures

To bring in Positive Energy to the home or dwelling.

Cleanse and to dispel any Negative Energies.

Prepare Smudge as mention before using one or all of Sacred Plants. The most common Plant Medicines for this purpose are Sage and Sweet Grass.

Open window or door a small amount to allow Negative Energy to escape the house or building.

An **Abalone Shell or Bowl** is usually used to place Plant Medicines* into.

Place Sacred Plant(s) into the Abalone Shell.

Sage - Cedar - Sweet Grass - Tobacco
(Can be used together or on their own)

After lighting Smudge you can Smudge yourself and anyone present.

Starting Smudge at the Main entrance.

Prayer can be said at the Main entrance or while Smudging the Home.

Say a Prayer asking the Creator to send Blessings to yourself, people there and to Bless the home.

You may ask the Creator's Love to enter the home and bring in good Positive Energy.

You can be specific in what you request.

Ask for Healing, Protection, Compassion, Guidance, Love, Family Unity and Harmony, Cleansing of the Home or of a particular Person to be Cleansed or Healed.

Pray for what is needed in a Good Way.

After Smudging yourself and others, proceed to Smudge in a clockwise direction through the Home.

Utilize the Feather to Brush Sacred Smoke into All corners of the Home.

Smudge all Rooms, closets, walls and spaces and all Sacred Items or Items of significance.

Make your way back to the Main entrance where you started.

SACRED SMUDGE

CEREMONY PRAYERS

Preceding Prayers

You may face the Spiritual Direction in which you are Praying.

These Prayers are meant as a guide. You are encouraged to have and say your own personal Prayers that have meaning to yourself and others.

Creator the Great Mystery …

We give Thanks to All Life that has been created.

Creator to smile upon us. We are kind to the Creators Spiritual Beings, the Animals, the Plants and all Creations.

We thank you for our Gift of Knowledge to live Healthy and in Balance with this World.

Bring forth your Energy to heal us and to Guide us.

To show us Harmony and Cooperation with our Brothers and Sisters.

To show us how to express Generosity and Compassion to others.

Grandfather Sun: Thank you for our Shadow.

For that which is represented by our shadows is our Ancestors. They that protect and guide us are with us always.

We give thanks for the Creators life giving energy. Passed to the Four corners of the universe, the Sun then passes this Energy to the Four corners of Mother Earth to give life to all living things.

We regard this Light as the voice of the Creator.

Mother Earth: We give Thanks for all that is provided for us to Live.

We give thanks for the Plants, Animals, Waters and All things upon the Earth need for our survival.

We thank Mother Earth for our Food, Medicines, Clothing, Tools and Shelter.

Everything we need to survive here is provided by Mother Earth and the many Spiritual Beings upon Her.

Mother Earth can heal us simply by walking in Her presence of Nature. Walk with awareness, letting go of the days worries, appreciating your surroundings and all the sights and sounds of Nature.

Mother Earth will speak to us if we are tuned in and are receptive to our surroundings in Nature.

Strengthen your connection to Nature by being Mindful to Mother Earths gifts to us.

Spirit of the East Wind

We thank the high flying Eagle for showing us how to See things in a Wider Perspective.

To seek New Paths and Directions.

For showing us how to express Love to our families.

For carrying our message of Prayer up to the Creator.

We must set a good example for the young ones coming up to follow.

We give thanks for new beginnings and the renewal of Life.

We praise new learning with the Morning Star of Knowledge and understanding.

We give thanks to the Mouse for showing us how to focus on the days tasks.

We look upon the world with New, Fresh and Innocent Eyes like the Bear Cub emerging in the Spring.

This is a Morning time of the New: Learning, Knowledge, Directions, Beginnings and Rebirth.

A guiding Path in a time of Life Transition and Change.

We ask for our Physical Body to be Healthy. Have respect for your body: keep it healthy and fit. Be mindful of what you put within it and how you treat it and others.

We ask that we all have the capacity to be Earth People in Balance with Humankind, the Environment and Creatures upon Mother Earth.

We ask to See this World in as New Light. Let go of Negative Habits and Beliefs. Like the Squirrel we need to clean our tail of Burrs and Knots from time to time.

Daughter Brittni and Grandson Nico

Spirit of the South Wind

We give thanks to the Spirit of the Women.
Holding the Power of Giving Life.

We give thanks to the Mothers for their patience, understanding and guidance. They are the University of the People

Sacred Keepers of the Waters that are essential to Giving Life to all living things.

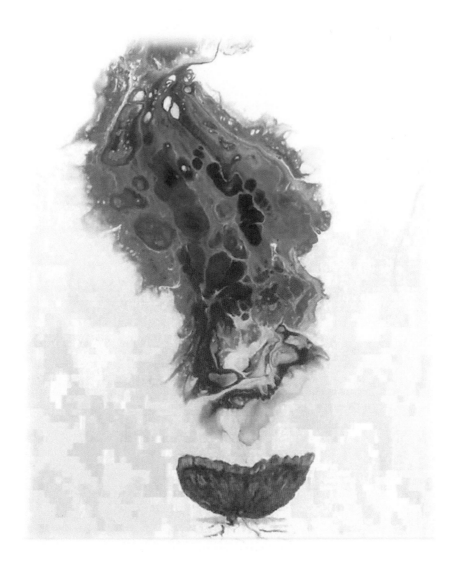

We give Thanks to the Spirit of Summer and its warm gentle winds that allows our Hearts to Smile.

To be vulnerable and express our feelings.

The South reminds us to release harmful negative feelings and have Kindness of Heart.

The Deer reminds us to carry ourselves with Grace and Dignity. To have Purity of Heart and Innocence.

The Spirit of the South shows us to have Harmony within our relationships with our partners. To have relationships founded on mutual respect.

At this time of warm season we are mindful of the Air, the Breath of Life: we take in Positive Energy and expel out the Negative.

We ask in Faith for that in which cannot be described. Humility is to admit there are things beyond our understanding. It requires Courage to have Faith in the Great Mystery.

We look to the Coyote to preserve our sense of Laughter. We consider Laughter one of the most powerful forms of Medicine. We often take ourselves too seriously and Coyote reminds us we are an essential drop of Water in a Big Ocean.

Spirit of the West Wind

We look to the Spirit of the West Wind for Spiritual: Guidance, Knowledge, and Moral Values.

Grandmothers and Grandfathers are the University of the People, passing down their Wisdom, Teachings, Language and Moral knowledge to Grandchildren at this time.

Respecting the Spirit of others. When speaking to others: ask yourself, am I being respectful to their and my Spirit.

We seek the guidance of the Bear to teach us the proper Medicines and how to Honor them.

We ask the Spirit Bear to help us to understand and remember our Dreams.

The Thunderbird of the Western Mountains nests in the Boughs of the Cedar Tree. We look to Cedar to dispel any Bad Dreams we may have. To protect our homes from strong storms.

As Evening falls and the Stars emerge we are reminded of the beginning of the Universe.

We give Thanks to our Spiritual Helpers and of our ancestors in the Spiritual Realm.

Spirit of the North Wind

We look to the Spirit of the North Wind for our Mental well-being.

To give us Focus, Maturity, Wisdom, Knowledge. We ask for good memory, organizational attributes and Clarity.

We ask for Comprehension that it vital to Interpretation and Understanding.

This is the time in Life to prepare for our next cycle of Life. It is a time to seek Reflection on our Life.

To Contemplate on our Life and think about the Legacy of Knowledge we pass down to the young ones.

The Spirit of the Buffalo, the great Provider and Nourisher to the People, shows us to be generous and to provide for those in need.

We look to the mighty Buffalo to remind us to show respect for our Elders.

Buffalo song reminds us to have strength and perseverance. To have Endurance and Purity.

The Northern Lights in the North Sky reminds us to acknowledge our Ancestors.

It is said that the **Light is the Voice of the Creator**.

We seek to strengthen our Intellectual Beliefs for Freedom and Justice.

We look to the Spirit of the North to seek Forgiveness for ourselves and towards others.

Individual ~ Home

Circle Prayer

Creator; we ask you to send Blessings to (Person or Place).

We ask for the Love of the Creator to enter this (Home or Space).

Creator: We ask to bring in good Positive Energy and to dispel all Bad Energies.

Great Spirit, we ask help for ourselves or loved ones. (Help these people for their specific need).

My Wife Tanya, Daughter Sylka and Son Dominic

Keep watch over our loved ones. Our Parents and Grandparents, our children, brothers and sisters.

Make sure they are safe and have good health.

We pray that the people here today stay safe and have good health.

We pray for the sick today. That the Creator help and heal them Physically, Emotionally, Spiritually and help them Think in a good way.

We ask for Healing, Protection, Compassion, Guidance and Love.

We ask for Family Unity and Harmony.

We ask for Cleansing of the Home of Negative Spiritual Energies.

We ask for (a particular Person) to be Cleansed or Healed.

We Pray for what is needed in a Good Way.

We give thanks for theses (things/people we value)

in our Life.

SPIRITUAL PROTOCOLS
Advice on Traditional Protocols.

You do not stand alone when Smudging. You stand with your Grandparents, your relatives, your Guardian Spiritual Helpers and with the Creator.

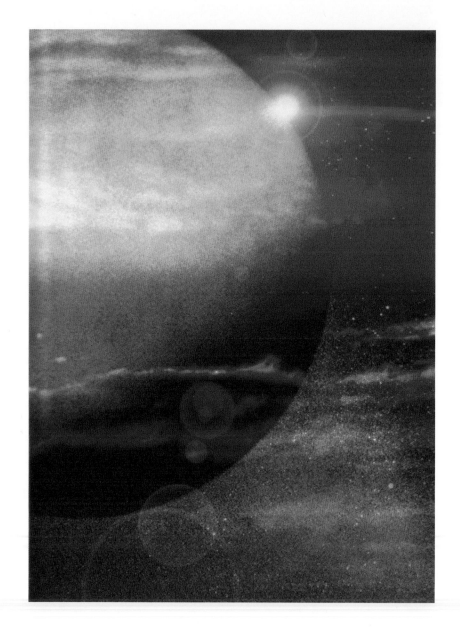

We keep it in mind to be Respectful and Mindful of your words and behavior around Sacred Ceremonial Items, Elements of Mother Earth and Plant Medicines.

Never step over Sacred Ceremonial Items and Medicines. Keep and Store with great respect.

It is not wise to blow on Fire as it may bring strong weather.

Sacrifice was made for Humankind to possess Fire.

Have respectful behavior when around all Fire.

Do not place waste into Ceremonial Fire.

Be sure to be in a positive and healthy place and state of mind to smudge.

A Positive state is very beneficial for healthy results.

We are not to swear, it not only offends people there, you do not stand alone when Smudging. You stand with your Grandparents, your relatives, your Guardian Spiritual Helpers and with the Creator.

Not to have bad thoughts of others. Smudging promotes having a positive outlook on your day ahead.

Respect the Circle and others, do not walk off, be distracted or have unnecessary talking.

ABOUT THE AUTHOR

Anishinnabe Cree Native
Traditional Firekeeper & Spiritualist
Writer, Speaker, Musician,
Spiritual Traditional Artist
Animikii Binesii ~ Twirling Thunderbird

Traditional Firekeeper & Spiritualist
Healing Sweat Lodge Facilitator
Knowledge Keeper
Native Traditional Artist
Published Writer ~ Musician ~ Public Speaker

First Nations Anishinaabe Cree
I'm a proud member of the Sapotaweyak Cree Nation
Manitoba, Canada

I receive great fulfillment in walking the
Path of Native Spirituality
within the Light of the Great Spirit.
I also enjoy giving back to the Creator for the Gift of Art
by facilitating as Firekeeper within Healing Sweat Lodge.

As a Musician I create my own Cedar Flutes
that I enjoy playing at Healing Lodge Ceremony.
As a Public Speaker I work to share Traditional Knowledge with Students.
They are the ones to carry the next torch forward.

As a self-taught Artist; I paint Spiritual Traditional Native Art,
Traditional Spiritual Pictographs, Abstract Art,
Expressionism, Landscapes, Wildlife Art,
Surreal Art, Watercolor, Graphic Design and Illustration.

My work has appeared in the
Pre-Calculus 12 Math Textbook
Distributed across Canada by
McGraw-Hill Ryerson Limited.

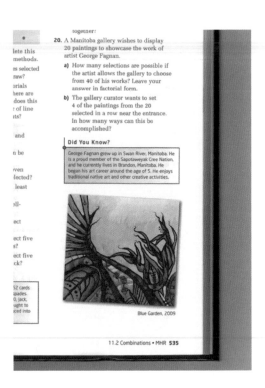

together:

20. A Manitoba gallery wishes to display 20 paintings to showcase the work of artist George Fagnan.

a) How many selections are possible if the artist allows the gallery to choose from 40 of his works? Leave your answer in factorial form.

b) The gallery curator wants to set 4 of the paintings from the 20 selected in a row near the entrance. In how many ways can this be accomplished?

Did You Know?

George Fagnan grew up in Swan River, Manitoba. He is a proud member of the Sapotaweyak Cree Nation, and he currently lives in Brandon, Manitoba. He began his art career around the age of 5. He enjoys traditional native art and other creative activities.

Blue Garden, 2009

11.2 Combinations • MHR **535**

As a writer, I am very proud of this published book
"Native American Smudge Guide Book"

As a Knowledge Keeper I work with Students teaching
Native Cultural Practices.
I value the Responsibility in passing knowledge
to the next generation.

"Thank You for reading my book.
I'm extremely grateful to share my knowledge with you.

I sincerely hope it brings you
Happiness and Health."

The Path of the Great Mystery

The Material World and The Spiritual Universe

I believe we are all interconnected to a "Source" or spiritual energy. There is a Spiritual World that we have the potential to experience.

Perception

Native Culture teaches there are two sides to everything that we know and experience.

People, Animals, Plants, objects, everything... All have a Spiritual side and a Physical material side.

What we think of as matter and space is not the full picture of the material world.

The known Universe is occupied by many other dimensions and many other "spiritual planes".

Matter itself is more than a vibration of energy. It has within, a Source Energy from the Creator.

The Physical side of the Universe, All living things, everything in the Universe; all have the Source Energy within.

All humans have a connection on a spiritual level within our consciousness to the spiritual plane.

Our Conscious Energy, when vibrating in Positive Synchronicity, can influence and promote Healing.

We often see the Creators Energy manifest in nature through symbiotic relationships, Biological Design, phenomenon such as instincts, human emotions, intuition and creativity.

Native culture teaches that this world we live in is but a shadow or reflection of the other larger spiritual world.

This spiritual plane or "other side" is alluded to by many cultures and religions.

We all have a shared connection to the Creator's Spiritual Energy and knowing that, we are all connected and part of a larger Universal consciousness.

Everything on this Earth, The Galaxy, and the whole of the Universe are connected.

We are spiritually connected to our fellow human Spiritual Beings, connected to the Animal, Plants and all that is on Mother Earth.

I once told my son to imagine that the Lamp light was the Creators Source Energy and the Shade when poked with small holes represented Living life-forms.

Although the pin holes of light had an Individual nature, they all came from the Creators Source.

The Creators Energy comes in many forms.

One of those being Love.

We have all experienced the Spiritual connection between our Mother and ourselves.

This is the Creator's connection.

Animikii Binesii

Twirling Thunderbird

Medicine Wheel

East Spirit
Element ~ Earth
Time ~ Morning
Season ~ Spring
Medicine ~ Tobacco
Stage ~ Baby
Place ~ Physical
Spirit ~ Eagle, Mouse,
Bear Cub

North Spirit
Element ~ Fire
Time ~ Night
Season ~ Winter
Medicine ~ Sweet Grass
Stage ~ Elder
Place ~ Mental
Spirit ~ Buffalo, Owl

South Spirit
Element ~ Air
Time ~ Noon
Season ~ Summer
Medicine ~ Sage
Stage ~ Youth
Place ~ Emotional
Spirit ~ Deer, Wolf,
Water Birds

West Spirit
Element ~ Water
Time ~ Evening
Season ~ Fall
Medicine ~ Cedar
Stage ~ Grandparent
Place ~ Spiritual
Spirit ~ Bear, Thunderbird, Turtle

TwirlingThunderbird.ca

Twirling Thunderbird

Smudging has for centuries been a source of
Healing and Cleansing.

The Self-Help guide book covers

- The Smudge Ceremony procedures, different types of Smudging Ceremonies. Individual, Family, Group Circle.

- What Plants are Utilized (Sage, Tobacco, Sweet Grass, and Cedar) and their Meaning within the Medicine Wheel.

- I also cover which Smudge Stick plants can be used for Smudging.

- Essential Oils that are used in Smudging.

- The meaning of the Feather and the Abalone Shell. Spiritual aspects.

- What to include in a Spiritual Ceremonial Prayer. Reasoning behind the Ceremony.

- The Power of Silence.

- The Power of Positive Vibrational. Creating Positive Space.

- Ceremony Protocols. Guidance and Advice on Smudging.

- Advice on clearing your living space of any negative or bad Spirits.

- Within this Guide book I offer my personal Smudge advice for beginners and advice towards the Sacred Smudging Ceremony.

- Expressing the Creators Gifts to find greater meaning and happiness in life.

- To seek balance within the Traditional Medicine Wheel and to receive Physical, Emotional, Spiritual and Mental well-being.

- We Smudge to promote a healthy Lifestyle.

- We honor the Healing Gifts of the Gitche Manitou - Great Mystery through sharing and strengthening our connection to our Environment.

- We encourage empathy and understanding to our fellow Spiritual Beings.

- For centuries many cultures have used smudging within the Family. Smudging is a way to create a cleansing smoke bath that is used to purify the body.

- To Re-Energize the Light Energy of our Aura.

- Promote Energy flow throughout the Body.

- To Purify and cleanse ceremonial/ritual spaces and any other Sacred space or personal objects.

I hope my personal advice on Smudge Ceremony will bring Happiness and Health.

I believe Ceremonial Smudge will I believe will always bring Goodness as long as it comes from the Heart with good intentions.

We are all born with Healing Gifts from the Creator.

I believe to share our Healing Gifts with others is the Key to personal Fulfillment and Happiness.

~ Twirling Thunderbird ~ Thank You ~ Megwetch

Twirling Thunderbird

Printed in Great Britain
by Amazon

5b964f0d-f787-4cce-811f-b9cc66d85d11R01